SALADS AND SALAD DRESSINGS

Salads are divided into two groups, dinner salads and the more substantial ones served at supper and luncheon in the place of meats. They are exceedingly wholesome.

Nearly all the meats, vegetables, and fruits may be served as salads. The essential thing is to have the salad fresh and cold; and if green, to have the leaves crisp and dry.

Lettuce, Romaine, endive and chicory or escarole make the best dinner salads, although one may use mixed cooked vegetables or well-prepared uncooked cabbage.

Left-over green vegetables, string beans, peas, carrots, turnips, cauliflower, cooked spinach, leeks and beets may all take their place in the dinner salad. Use them mixed, alone, or as a garnish for lettuce.

Lettuce and all green, raw salad vegetables should be washed and soaked in cold water as soon as they come from the market. After they have stood fifteen to twenty minutes in cold or ice water, free them from moisture by swinging them in a wire basket, or dry, without bruising, each leaf carefully with a napkin. Put them in a cheese-cloth bag and on the ice, ready for service. In this way they will remain dry and cold, and will keep nicely for a week.

The dressing is added only at the moment of serving, as the salad wilts if allowed to stand after the dressing is added.

Meat of any kind used for salads should be cut into dice, but not smaller than one-half inch, or it will seem like hash. It should be marinated before being mixed with the other parts of the salad. Meat mixtures are usually piled in cone-shape on a dish, the mayonnaise then spread over it, and garnished with lettuce, capers, hard-boiled eggs, gherkins, etc.

To Marinate.—Take one part of oil and three of vinegar, with pepper and salt for taste; stir them into the meat, and let it stand a couple of hours; drain off any of the marinade which has not been absorbed before combining the meat with the other parts of the salad. Use only enough marinade to season the meat or fish.

If too much vinegar is added to mayonnaise it robs it of its consistency and flavor. All salads must be mixed at the last minute, at serving time. Mayonnaise dressing may be made hours before and the meat, lettuce and celery prepared, but each must be kept in a separate dish until mixing time.

SALAD DRESSINGS

MAYONNAISE DRESSING

Beat the yolk of one egg in a cold dish with a silver or wooden fork. If the weather is very warm, place the bowl in a larger vessel filled with chopped ice. When the egg is beaten add one-half teaspoon of salt, dash of red pepper, one-half teaspoon of English mustard and olive oil, drop by drop, being careful to beat well without reversing the motion for fear of curdling. When the dressing thickens, begin adding the vinegar or lemon juice, drop by drop. Then add more olive oil, then more acid, continuing until one cup of olive oil and two teaspoons of vinegar or lemon juice are all used. Be sure to have all the ingredients and dishes as cold as possible.

If the mixture should curdle, begin immediately with a fresh egg in a fresh dish and when it is well beaten add carefully the curdled mixture, drop by drop.

To serve twenty people one pint of mayonnaise is required.

MAYONNAISE WITH WHIPPED CREAM

When you are in want of a large quantity of dressing, mayonnaise or French, add one pint of whipped cream to your prepared dressing, stirring thoroughly, just before ready to serve.

COLORED MAYONNAISE

To color mayonnaise, chop parsley leaves very fine; pound them in a small quantity of lemon juice; strain and add the juice to the dressing.

WHITE MAYONNAISE

To make white mayonnaise, follow the ordinary directions, using lemon juice instead of vinegar, omitting the mustard and adding, when finished, a half cup of whipped cream or half an egg white beaten very stiff.

STUFFED TOMATOES, CHEESE SALAD

Wash and skin six small tomatoes. Cut a piece from the stem end of each and when cold remove a portion of the pulp from the centre. Then sprinkle with salt and invert on the ice to chill. Mash to a paste one small cream cheese add two tablespoons of chopped pimento, one tablespoon of French mustard. Blend well, moisten with a French dressing and fill into the tomato shells. Arrange on a bed of crisp lettuce leaves and pour over each tomato a tablespoon of thick boiled dressing.

LIMA BEAN SALAD

Take two cups of cold, cooked Lima beans, two stalks of chopped celery, one dozen chopped olives, one teaspoon of onion juice, one teaspoon of salt, and a dash of red pepper. Mix thoroughly and serve on lettuce leaves with French dressing and garnish with green and red peppers cut in squares.

PEPPER AND CHEESE SALAD

Fill green peppers with a mixture of cream cheese and chopped olives. Set on the ice and then slice the peppers and serve a slice (shaped like a four-leaf clover) on a leaf of lettuce. Small brown bread sandwiches go well with this.

GREEN PEPPERS FOR SALAD

Put whole, green sweet pepper in boiling water and cook until tender. Place on platter and drain. Make a dressing of vinegar, salt, sugar and oil. Serve.

PEPPER SALAD

Cut the peppers lengthwise in half, and fill with a mixture of flaked, cold cooked fish and minced celery, mixed with mayonnaise.

POTATO SALAD, No. 1

Boil ten potatoes (small, round ones preferred) in their skins. When done, peel them while, still hot and slice in thin, round slices. Spread over the potatoes one onion, sliced fine, and sprinkle generously with salt and pepper, add one tablespoon of mustard seed, one-half tablespoon of celery seed, and one-half tablespoon of sugar.

Beat one egg until light, pour two tablespoons of goose or chicken fat, melted, over the eggs, stir well, add one-half cup of vinegar, pour over the seasoned potatoes: then add one-quarter cup of hot water and if necessary, add a little more vinegar, salt or pepper. One or two chopped hard-boiled eggs added improves the salad. Line a salad bowl with lettuce leaves, pour in the salad and decorate the top with grated hard-boiled eggs.

Melted butter may be used if for a milk meal or heated olive oil for a parve salad in place of the melted fat.

POTATO SALAD, No. 2

Boil one quart of small potatoes, Bermuda potatoes are best. Do not peel them, just wash and scrub the potatoes thoroughly in cold water. Put them in a kettle with enough cold water, slightly salted, just to cover them; stand them over a brisk fire with the kettle covered until the water begins to boil; then turn down the heat, lift the cover of the kettle slightly and let the potatoes cook slowly till done. Drain off the water and stand the potatoes where they will get cold. But do not put them in a refrigerator. When quite cold, peel the potatoes and slice them very thin in a salad bowl. To every two layers of potato slices sprinkle over a very light layer of white onions sliced very thin. Texas onions are particularly fine for this purpose.

When the salad bowl is well filled pour over the salad a French dressing made of equal parts of oil and vinegar; let the vinegar be part tarragon; use a palatable amount of salt and pepper. When ready to serve, cover the surface of the salad with a stiff mayonnaise in which a suggestion of cream has been mixed. Ornament with quarters of hard-boiled eggs, boiled beets cut in fancy slices and a fringe of parsley around the edge of the bowl.

POTATO SALAD, No. 3

Put into a bowl two tablespoons of olive oil, one tablespoon of sugar, one teaspoon of salt, some pepper and one tablespoon of vinegar and mix all together. Cut into this in slices six hot potatoes. Then cut into small pieces two small onions, a little garlic, some parsley, six stuffed olives, three hearts of celery (or the end of it), six radishes, three slices of red beets and two hard-boiled eggs. Add this to the gravy in the bowl, mix well, and season to taste. Put all into a glass dish and pour over this a prepared mayonnaise dressing. Decorate with parsley, olives (whole), some lettuce and put in the centre some celery leaves.

SQUASH SALAD (TURKISH STYLE)

Grate off the skin of long squash (the kind that looks like cucumbers), cut the squash in slices, one-quarter of an inch thick, and fry in olive oil; prepare a sauce with a little vinegar, one-half teaspoon of prepared mustard, two tablespoons of olive oil, beat these ingredients very well; add two shallots or leeks, cut in small pieces, pour sauce over the squash and serve.

WALDORF SALAD

Mix an equal quantity of sliced celery and apples, and a quarter of a pound of pecans or English walnuts, chopped fine. Put over a tablespoon of lemon juice and sufficient mayonnaise dressing to thoroughly cover. To be absolutely correct, this salad should be served without lettuce; it can, however, be dished on lettuce leaves.

WATER-LILY SALAD

Boil twenty minutes, one egg for each lily; remove shell and while still warm cut with silver knife in strips from small end nearly to base; very carefully lay back the petals on a heart of bleached lettuce; remove yolks and rub them with spoon of butter, vinegar, a little mustard, salt and paprika; form cone-shaped balls, and put on petals, sprinkling bits of parsley over balls. Two or three stuffed olives carry out the effect of buds; serve on cut-glass dishes to give water effect.

MARSHMALLOW SALAD

Cut up one-quarter pound of marshmallows into small squares, also contents of one-half can of pineapple. Let the marshmallows be mixed with the pineapples quite a while before salad is put together; add to this one-quarter pound of shelled pecans. Make a drip mayonnaise of one yolk of egg into which one-half cup of oil is stirred drop by drop; cut this with lemon juice, but do not use any sugar; to two tablespoons of mayonnaise, add four tablespoons of whipped cream. Serve on fresh, green lettuce-leaves.

COTTAGE CHEESE SALAD

Mix thoroughly one pound of cheese, one and one-half tablespoons of cream, one tablespoon of chopped parsley and salt to taste. First fill a rectangular tin mold with cold water to chill and wet the surface; line the bottom with waxed paper, then pack in three layers, putting two or three parallel strips of pimento between layers. Cover with waxed paper and set in a cool place until ready to serve; then run a knife around the sides and invert the mold. Cut in slices and serve on lettuce leaves with French dressing and wafers. Minced olives may be used instead of the parsley, and chopped nuts also may be added.

CREAM CHEESE SALAD

Moisten a cream cheese with cream and beat to a froth. Arrange in a mound shape on a dish and turn preserved gooseberries over it. Serve with biscuits.

CREAM CHEESE SALAD WITH PINEAPPLES

Serve one slice of Hawaiian pineapple on lettuce leaves. On the pineapple slice place a spoon of cream cheese and some chopped walnuts and top off with a dash of mayonnaise dressing.

FRUIT SALAD

Slice one pineapple, three oranges, and three bananas. Pour over it a French mayonnaise, put on lettuce leaves and serve at once. For those who do not care for the mayonnaise, make a syrup of one cup of sugar and one-half cup of water, boil until thick, add juice of lemon, let slightly cool, then pour over fruit. Let stand on ice one to two hours. Another nice dressing is one cup of claret, one-half cup of sugar, and piece of lemon. Always use lemon juice in preference to vinegar in fruit salads. All fruits that go well together may be mixed. This is served just before desert.

FRUIT AND NUT SALAD

Slice two bananas, two oranges and mix them with one-half cup of English walnuts and the juice of one-half lemon with French dressing. Serve on lettuce leaves.

GRAPE-FRUIT SALAD

Cut the grape-fruit in halves and remove the pulp, being careful to get none of the tough white skin. Mix with bananas and oranges and stir in white mayonnaise dressing. Remove all skin from the inside, of the grape-fruit and fill with the mixture, heaping it high and ornamenting with maraschino cherries. Lay each half in a bed of lettuce leaves and serve.

BANANA DAINTY

Cut the bananas in half crosswise and arrange them on a plate, radiating from the center. Sprinkle with grated nuts or nutmeg and heap white mayonnaise in the center. Garnish with maraschino cherries.

HUNGARIAN FRUIT SALAD

Mix together equal parts of banana, orange, pineapple, grapefruit and one-half cup of chopped nuts. Marinate with French dressing. Fill apple or orange skins with mixture. Arrange on a bed of watercress or lettuce leaves. Sprinkle with paprika.

NUT SALAD

Make a plain grape-fruit salad. When you have it ready to serve, cover the top thickly with finely chopped almonds or pecans mixed. Pour over French dressing.

RUSSIAN FRUIT SALAD

Peel and pit some peaches, cut in slices and add as much sliced pineapple, some apricots, strawberries and raspberries, put these in a dish. Prepare a syrup of juice of two lemons, two oranges, one cup of water and one pound sugar, a half teaspoon of powdered cinnamon, grated rind of lemon, add one cup red wine and a half glass of Madeira, arrak or rum. Boil this syrup for five minutes, then pour over the fruit, tossing the fruit from time to time until cool. Place on ice and serve cold.

FISH SALAD

Take one pound cold boiled fish left over from the day previous, or boil fresh fish and let cool, then skin, bone and flake. If fresh fish is used, mix two tablespoons of vinegar, a pinch of salt and pepper with the fish. Make a mayonnaise dressing (French mayonnaise preferred), and mix half with the fish, leaving other half to spread over top of salad, after it is put in bowl. Serve either with or without lettuce leaves.

FISH SALAD FOR TWENTY PEOPLE

Boil four pounds of halibut, cool and shred fish. Marinate the fish as directed. When ready to serve add six hard-boiled eggs chopped, and one pint bottle of pickles or chow-chow. The pickle may be omitted and celery cut fine be added. When these are well mixed serve on lettuce leaves with mayonnaise dressing, of which one pint will be required.

MAYONNAISE OF FLOUNDER

Put some fillets of flounder into boiling water with a little salt and lemon juice, and cook until tender, then drain thoroughly.

When cold, put them in the center of some chopped lettuce, cover with mayonnaise sauce and garnish with slices of tomatoes and hard-boiled eggs.

HERRING SALAD, No. 1

Soak four herrings in cold water overnight, and then rinse several times in fresh cold water. Skin, bone, and cut in one-half inch pieces. Peel two apples, and cut in dice. Mix with herring, then add one-half cup of coarsely chopped almonds and one onion chopped fine. Remove the milsner or soft egg from the inside of herring, and mash perfectly smooth. Add one-half cup of vinegar, one teaspoon of sugar, pinch of pepper. Mix well, and then pour over herring, stirring with a fork to prevent mashing. Set in ice-box until ready to serve. Put sliced lemons on top. Herring can be left whole, dressing made and poured over whole herrings.

HERRING SALAD, No. 2

Soak three nice herrings in cold water three hours. Then remove the head and tail and bones. With a scissors cut in pieces as small as dice, add one-half cup of English walnuts cut fine, one tablespoon of boiled beets cut fine, two tablespoons of capers, one large apple cut in small pieces and one dill pickle cut up. Then take the soft egg (milchner) and mix with two cups of white vinegar until soft, add one teaspoon of sugar, three cloves and allspice and pour the sauce over the ingredients. The sauce should not be too thick. Mix all well together, and serve a spoonful on a lettuce leaf for each person.

This salad will keep for weeks.

HUNGARIAN VEGETABLE SALAD

Mix together one cup each of cold cooked peas, beans, carrots, and potatoes. Cover with French dressing and let stand for twenty minutes. Add one cup of smoked salmon or haddock, cut in small pieces, the chopped whites of four hard-boiled eggs and two stalks of celery. Mix thoroughly, garnish top with yolk of egg pressed through a wire sieve; and with cucumbers and beets, cut in fancy shapes.

SALMON SALAD

Either cold boiled salmon or the canned variety may be used. In the latter event wash the fish, in cold water, drain and expose to the outside air for at least one hour, as this removes any suggestion of the can. Flake the fish into small particles and to each cupful of the fish add the same quantity of shredded lettuce, one coarsely chopped hard-boiled egg, three slices of minced cucumber and six chopped olives. Mix the ingredients well, moisten with either a mayonnaise or boiled dressing and serve in individual portions in nest of heart lettuce leaves. Mask each portion with a tablespoon of dressing and garnish with capers and grated egg yolk.

MAYONNAISE ESPECIALLY FOR SALMON

Rub the yolks of two hard-boiled eggs to a powder, then add eight tablespoons of cream very gradually to them, also white pepper, a pinch of salt and a mere suspicion of cayenne pepper. Lastly add two tablespoons of white vinegar. It is very important that this last ingredient be put in drop by drop, otherwise the mixture will curdle.

MACKEREL SALAD

Procure a nice fat mackerel, boil, and when cold, proceed same as for "Salmon Salad," only do not cut the pieces quite as small.

MONTEREY SALAD

Select fine lemons, wipe carefully, scoop out the pulp, remove the tough inner skin and seeds, and to the rest add one box of boneless sardines, finely chopped, one teaspoon of French mustard, two hard-boiled eggs chopped, some tabasco sauce, and mayonnaise. Fill each cup with the mixture. Cut a small slice from the bottom of the lemon, so that it will stand firmly. Garnish with chopped egg and chopped parsley, and serve on lettuce leaves.

RUSSIAN SALAD

Cut up all kinds of pickled cucumbers, small and large, sweet and sour, also (senf) mustard pickles, into very small lengths, also pickled beans and capers. Add six herring, which you have soaked in water for twenty-four hours; skin and take out every bone, cut up as you did the pickles. Add half a pound of smoked salmon, also cut into lengths, six large apples chopped very fine, and one onion grated; mix all thoroughly and pour a rich mayonnaise dressing over all. Next day line a salad bowl with lettuce leaves, fill in the salad and garnish with hard-boiled eggs, nuts, and capers.

NIAGARA SALAD

Pick or grind one thick slice of cold, cooked salmon. Make a dressing of mayonnaise, to which add one tablespoon of French mustard, one green onion chopped fine, one tablespoon of small Mexican peppers, one tablespoon of pimentos. Mix this dressing into the picked salmon.

CHICKEN SALAD

Place the chicken in boiling water, add one onion, a bay leaf and six cloves. Bring to a boil and let it boil rapidly for five minutes. Reduce the heat to below the boiling point, and let it cook until tender. Let chicken cool in the broth.

By cooking it in this manner the dark meat will be almost as white as the meat of the breast. When the chicken is cold, cut into half inch cubes, removing all the fat and skin. To each pint allow one tablespoon of lemon juice, sprinkle the latter over the prepared chicken and place on ice. When ready to serve, mix the chicken with two-thirds as much white celery, cut into corresponding pieces: meanwhile prepare the following mayonnaise: Rub the yolks of two hard-boiled eggs as fine as possible, add one teaspoon of salt, then add, a drop at a time, one teaspoon of the finest olive oil. Stir constantly, add one teaspoon of prepared mustard and while pepper, and two teaspoons of white sugar; whip the white of one egg to a froth and add to the dressing; add about one-half cup of vinegar last, a spoonful at a time. Put the salad into the dressing carefully, using two silver forks; line the salad bowl with lettuce leaves, and garnish the top with the whites of hard-boiled eggs chopped up, or cut into half-moons. Garnish this salad with the chopped yolks and whites of hard-boiled eggs, being careful to have the whites and yolks separate. A few olives and capers will add to the decoration.

CHICKEN SALAD FOR TWENTY PEOPLE

Boil two large chickens in enough water to cover them, add salt while boiling; when very tender remove from the fire and allow the chickens to cool in the liquor in which they were boiled, when cold skim off every particle of fat, and reserve it to use instead of oil. If possible boil the chickens the day previous to using. Now cut the chickens up into small bits (do not chop), cut white, crisp celery in half inch pieces, and sprinkle with fine salt, allowing half as much celery as you have chicken, mixing the chicken and celery, using two silver forks to do this. Rub the yolks of six hard-boiled eggs as fine as possible, add one-half teaspoon of salt, white pepper, four tablespoons of chicken-fat that has been skimmed off the broth, adding one at a time, stirring constantly, one tablespoon of best prepared mustard, two teaspoons each mustard seed and celery seed, and two tablespoons of white sugar; add gradually, stirring constantly, one cup of white wine vinegar. Pour this dressing over the chicken and celery and toss lightly with the silver forks. Line a large salad bowl with lettuce leaves, pour in the salad and garnish the top with the chopped whites of six hard-boiled eggs; pour a pint of mayonnaise over the salad just before serving. A neat way is to serve the salad in individual salad dishes, lining each dish with a lettuce leaf, garnish the salad with an olive stuck up in the center of each portion.

The bones of the chicken may be used for soup, letting them simmer in water to cover for three hours.

BRAIN SALAD

Scald brains with boiling hot water to cleanse thoroughly. Boil until tender, in fresh cold salt water, being careful to remove from water while it is yet firm. Slice lengthwise and lay in dish. Pour over one-half cup of vinegar, which has been sweetened with a pinch of sugar to remove sharp taste, pinch of salt and pepper. Garnish with parsley and serve cold. Can also be served with mayonnaise.

SWEETBREAD SALAD

Take cucumbers and cut lengthwise to serve the salad in; scrape out the inside and salt well, then squeeze and use this to mix with the filling. Take a pair of sweetbreads, or calf's brains, wash well, and boil; when done, throw in cold water at once and skim them; chop fine, add bunch of celery (if you can get it), one can of French peas, scraped part of cucumber; mix all together and season. Make a mayonnaise, mix with it, and fill the cucumber shells; keep all cold, and serve on lettuce leaf.

VEAL SALAD

Cut cold veal in half-inch slices, season with two tablespoons of vinegar, pinch of salt and pepper. Make a dressing using the yolks of three hard-boiled eggs, mashed smooth, add gradually two tablespoons of melted cold chicken or turkey grease, stir until smooth and thick, then add one teaspoon of prepared mustard, large pinch of salt and pepper, one teaspoon of sugar, one teaspoon each of mustard and celery seed, and five tablespoons of white vinegar. Mix the dressing well with the veal, and serve with or without lettuce leaves.

NEAPOLITAN SALAD

Take some white meat of a turkey, cut up fine, cut up a few pickles the same way, a few beets, one or two carrots, a few potatoes (the carrots and potatoes must be parboiled), also a few stalks of asparagus; chop up a bunch of crisp, white celery; a whole celery root (parboiled), sprinkle all with fine salt and pour a mayonnaise dressing over it. Line the salad bowl with lettuce leaves or white cabbage leaves. Add a few hard-boiled eggs and capers; garnish with sprigs of fresh parsley.

POLISH SALAD, OR SALAD PIQUANT

Lay half a dozen or more large salt pickles in water for about six hours, then drain off all the water. Chop up two sour apples, one large onion or two small ones, chop the pickles and mix all thoroughly in a bowl and sprinkle over them a scant half teaspoon of pepper (white) and a tablespoon of sugar (either white or brown), adding a pinch of salt if necessary. Pour enough white wine vinegar over all to just cover. Do not make more at a time than you can use up in a week, as it will not keep longer.

FRESH FRUITS AND COMPOTE

Always select the best fruit, as it is the cheapest, and requires less sugar; and where every piece of fruit or every berry is perfect, there is no waste. Raspberries are apt to harbor worms and therefore the freshly picked berries are safest.

BLUEBERRIES

Wash and pick over carefully, drain off all the water, sprinkle powdered sugar over them and serve with cream or milk.

RASPBERRIES

Pick over carefully, set on ice, and serve in a dish unsugared. Strawberries may be served as above.

RASPBERRIES AND CURRANTS

These berries, mixed, make a very palatable dish. Set on ice until ready to serve. Then pile in a mound, strewing plenty of pulverized sugar among them. As you do this, garnish the base with white or black currants (blackberries look pretty also) in bunches. Eat with cream or wine.

STRAWBERRIES

Pick nice ripe berries, pile them in a fruit dish. Strew plenty of pulverized sugar over them and garnish with round slices or quarters of oranges, also well sugared.

BANANAS

May be sliced according to fancy, either round or lengthwise. Set on ice until required. Then add sugar, wine or orange juice. In serving, dish out with a tablespoon of whipped cream.

CHILLED BANANAS

Cut ice-cold bananas down lengthwise, and lay these halves on a plate with a quarter of a lemon and a generous teaspoon of powdered sugar. Eat with a fork or spoon after sprinkling with lemon juice and dipping in sugar.

GRAPE FRUIT

Cut in half, with a sharp knife, remove seeds, and sprinkle with sugar, or loosen pulp; cut out pithy white centre; wipe knife after each cutting, so that the bitter taste may be avoided. Pour in white wine or sherry and sprinkle with powdered sugar, and let stand several hours in ice-chest to ripen. Serve cold in the shell. Decorate with maraschino cherry.

ORANGES

Cut an orange in half crosswise. Place on an attractive dish, scoop out the juice and pulp with a spoon and sweeten if necessary.

PINEAPPLE

Peel the pineapple, dig out all the eyes, then cut from the core downward, or chop in a chopping-bowl, and set on ice until ready to serve. Then sugar the fruit well, and form into a mound in a dish. Garnish the base well with leaves or small fruit of any kind. You may squeeze the juice of one orange over all.

PEACHES

Peel fine, ripe freestone peaches. Cover plentifully with pulverized sugar, and serve with whipped cream. The cream should be ice cold. Peaches should not be sliced until just before dining, or they will be very apt to change color.

WATERMELONS

Use only those melons that are perfectly ripe. Do not select those that are very large in circumference; a rough melon with a bumpy surface is the best. Either cut in half or plug and fill with the following: Put on to boil some pale sherry or claret and boil down to quite a thick syrup with sugar. Pour this into either a plugged melon or over the half-cut melon, and lay on ice for a couple of hours before serving. If you use claret you may spice it while boiling with whole spices.

SNOWFLAKES

Grate a large cocoanut into a fruit dish, and mix it thoroughly and lightly with pulverised sugar. Serve with whipped or plain sweet cream.

TUTTI-FRUTTI

Slice oranges, bananas, pineapples and arrange in a glass-bowl; sprinkle with pulverized sugar, and serve either with wine or cream. You may use both.

RIPE TOMATOES

Select nice, large, well-shaped tomatoes, pare, slice and put on ice. When ready to serve sprinkle each layer thickly with pulverized sugar.

PINEAPPLE SOUFFLÉ

Take a nice ripe pineapple, grate it and sweeten to taste. Beat the whites of two eggs stiff and mix with the pineapple. Before serving, whip half a pint of cream and put on the pineapple.

FROSTED APPLES

Pare and core six large apples. Cover with one pint of water and three tablespoons of sugar; simmer until tender. Remove from the syrup and drain. Wash the parings and let simmer with a little water for one-half hour. Beat the white of one egg to a stiff froth and add one tablespoon of sugar. Coat the top of the apples lightly with the meringue and place in a cool oven to dry. Strain the juice from the parings, add two tablespoons of sugar, return to the fire and let boil for five minutes; add a few drops of lemon juice and a little nutmeg, cool and pour around the apples.

APPLE FLOAT

Peel six big apples and slice them. Put them in a saucepan with just enough water to cover them and cook until tender. Then put them through a colander and add the grated rind and juice of half a lemon, sweeten to taste and stir in a trace of nutmeg. Fold in the stiffly beaten whites of four eggs and put the dish on ice. Serve with whipped or plain cream.

APPLE DELIGHT

Put a layer of apple sauce in a buttered pudding dish, dot with butter, add a layer of chopped peaches and apricots, sprinkle with blanched almonds ground rather coarsely, repeat until the pan is full; pour the peach juice over the mixture and bake for one hour.

APPLE COMPOTE

Take six apples ("Greenings," "Baldwins" or "Bellflowers"), pare, quarter, core and lay them in cold water as soon as pared. Then take the parings and seeds, put in a dish with a cup of water and a cup of white wine, and boil for about fifteen minutes. Strain through a fine sieve, then put on to boil again, and add half a cup of white sugar and the peel of half a lemon. Put in the apples and let them stew for fifteen minutes longer. When the apples are tender, take up each piece carefully with a silver spoon and lay on a platter to cool. Let the syrup boil down to about half the quantity you had after removing the apples, and add to it the juice of half a lemon. Lay your apples in a fruit dish, pyramid shape, pour the syrup over them, serve.

BAKED APPLES

Take large, juicy apples, wash and core them well, fill each place that you have cored with brown sugar, cinnamon and raisins, and put a clove in each apple. Lay them in a deep dish, pour a teacup of water in the dish, and put a little sugar on top of each apple. When well done the apples will be broken. Then remove them carefully to the dish they are to be served in and pour the syrup over them. To be eaten cold. If you wish them extra nice, glaze them with the beaten white of an egg, half a cup of pulverized sugar and serve with whipped cream.

STEAMED SWEET APPLES

For this dish use sweet apples, and steam in a closely covered iron pot for three-quarters of an hour.

Quarter and core five apples without paring. Put into the pot and melt beef drippings; when hot, lay a layer of apples in, skin down, sprinkle with brown sugar, and when nearly done, turn and brown; place on a platter and sprinkle with sugar.

FRIED APPLES

Quarter and core five apples without paring. Put into a frying-pan one cup of sugar, one tablespoon of butter and three tablespoons of water. Let this melt and lay in the apples with the skin up. Cover and fry slowly until brown.

APPLE SAUCE VICTORIA

Pare, quarter and core the apples. Set on to boil in cold water, and boil them over a very brisk fire; when they are soft mash with a potato masher and pass the mashed apples through a sieve. Sweeten to taste and flavor with a teaspoon of vanilla. This way of seasoning apples is highly recommended, especially if they are tasteless.

PEACH COMPOTE

Pare the fruit, leave it whole and put on to boil with sweetened water. Add a few cloves (remove the heads), also a stick of cinnamon bark. Boil the peaches until tender, then take up with a perforated skimmer and lay them in your fruit dish. Boil the syrup until thick, then pour over the peaches. Eat cold with sweet cream. Common cheap peaches make a very nice dessert, cooked in the above manner, clings especially, which cannot be used to cut up.

COMPOTE OF RASPBERRIES

Make a syrup of half a pound of sugar and half a cup of water, put into it one quart of berries which have been carefully picked and washed. Boil up once. Serve cold.

COMPOTE OF PINEAPPLE

Cut off the rind of a pineapple, core and trim out all the eyes. Cut into desired slices. Set on to boil with half a pound of sugar, and the juice of one or two tart oranges. When the pineapple is tender and clear, put into a compote dish and boil the syrup until clear. Pour over all and cool. The addition of a wineglass of brandy improves this compote very much.

COMPOTE OF PEARS

It is not necessary to take a fine quality of pears for this purpose. Pare the fruit, leaving on the stems, and stew in sugar and a very little water. Flavor with stick cinnamon and a few cloves (take out the head of each clove) and when soft place each pear carefully on a platter until cold. Then arrange them nicely in a glass bowl or flat glass dish, the stems all on the outer rim. Pour over them the sauce, which should be boiled thick like syrup. Eat cold.

HUCKLEBERRY COMPOTE

Pick over a quart of huckleberries or blueberries, wash them and set to boil. Do not add any water to them. Sweeten with half a cup of sugar, and spice with half a teaspoon of cinnamon. Just before removing from the fire, add a teaspoon of cornstarch which has been wet with a little cold water. Do this thoroughly in a cup and stir with a teaspoon so as not to have any lumps in it. Pour into a glass bowl. Eat cold.

RHUBARB SAUCE

Strip the skin off the stalks with care, cut them into small pieces, put into a saucepan with very little water, and stew slowly until soft. Sweeten while hot, but do not boil the sugar with the fruit. Eat cold. Very wholesome.

BAKED RHUBARB

Peel and cut into two-inch lengths three bunches of rhubarb. Dredge with flour and put in baking dish with one cup of sugar sprinkled over. Bake in moderate oven three-quarters of an hour. Very nice served hot as a vegetable, or cold as a sauce.

FIG SAUCE

Stew figs slowly for two hours, until soft; sweeten with loaf sugar, about two tablespoons to a pound of fruit; add a glass of port or other wine and a little lemon juice. Serve when cold.

DRIED FRUITS

To cook dried fruits thoroughly they should after careful washing be soaked overnight. Next morning put them over the fire in the water in which they have been soaked; bring to a boil; then simmer slowly until the fruit is thoroughly cooked but not broken. Sweeten to taste. Very much less sugar will be needed than for fresh fruit.

STEWED PRUNES

Cleanse thoroughly, soak in water ten or twelve hours, adding a little granulated sugar when putting to soak, for although the fruit is sweet enough, yet experience has shown that the added sugar changes by chemical process into fruit sugar and brings out better the flavor of the fruit. After soaking, the fruit will assume its full size, and is ready to be simmered on the back of the stove. Do not boil prunes, that is what spoils them. Simmer, simmer only. Keep lid on. Shake gently, do not stir, and never let boil. When tender they are ready for table. Serve cold, and a little cream will make them more delicious. A little claret or sauterne poured over the prunes just as cooking is finished adds a flavor relished by many. Added just before simmering, a little sliced lemon or orange gives a rich color and flavor to the syrup.

BAKED PRUNES

Cook prunes in an earthenware bean pot in the oven. Wash and soak the prunes and put them in the pot with a very little water; let them cook slowly for a long time. They will be found delicious, thick and rich, without any of the objectionable sweetness. Lemon, juice and peel, may be added if desired.

PRUNES WITHOUT SUGAR

Wash prunes thoroughly, pour boiling water over same and let them stand for ten minutes. Then drain and pour boiling water over them again; put in sealed jar; see that prunes are all covered with water. Ready for use after forty-eight hours. Will keep for a week at a time and the longer they stand the thicker the syrup gets.

STEAMED PRUNES

Steam until the fruit is swollen to its original size and is tender.
Sprinkle with powdered sugar and squeeze lemon juice over them.

PRUNE SOUFFLÉ

Remove the pits from a large cup of stewed prunes and chop fine. Add the whites of three eggs and a half cup of sugar beaten to a stiff froth. Mix well, turn into a buttered dish and bake thirty minutes in a moderate oven. Serve with whipped cream. If it is desired to cook this in individual cups, butter the cups, fill only two-thirds full, to allow for puffing up of the eggs, and set the cup a in a pan of water to bake. Some like a dash of cinnamon in this.

SWEET ENTRÉE OF RIPE PEACHES

Take large, solid peaches, pour boiling water over them so that the skin may be removed smoothly. Have ready thick syrup made of sugar and water. When boiling hot add peaches and boil about five minutes; remove and place in ice chest. When ready to serve have a sweet cracker on dish, place peach on same and pour over this a raspberry jelly slightly thinned and cover all with salted almonds or walnuts. Other fruits may be treated in like manner.

MEHLSPEISE (FLOUR FOODS)

NOODLES

Beat three whole eggs very light and sift in sufficient flour to make a stiff paste. Work until smooth, break off a piece and roll out on board very thin. Break oft another piece and roll and continue until all is used. Let rolled-out dough dry, then cut all except one piece in long strips one inch wide. Fold the one piece in layers and cut very fine noodles. Boil large noodles in pot of salted boiling water, drain in colander when tender and stir in two tablespoons of butter. Heat a tablespoon of butter in the frying-pan and brown fine noodles in this butter. Sprinkle these over the broad noodles, pour a cup of milk over the whole and brown in stove. Serve in same dish in which it was baked.

BROAD NOODLES

Make noodles as above and when drained sprinkle with fine noodles which have been browned in two tablespoons of sweet dripping; serve as a vegetable. If so desired, a cup of soup stock may be added and noodles browned in stove. Serve hot.

NOODLES WITH BUTTER

Plunge one pound of noodles into two quarts of boiling water and cook for fifteen minutes. Drain well, replace in the same pan, season with one-half teaspoon of salt, two teaspoons of white pepper, adding one ounce good butter. Gently mix without breaking the noodles until the butter is thoroughly dissolved, and serve.

NOODLES WITH CHEESE

If you make the noodles at home, use two eggs for the dough; if you buy macaroni use one-quarter of a pound, cut up and boil in salt water; boil about fifteen minutes; drain off the water and let cold water run through them; grate a cup of cheese; melt a piece of fresh butter, about the size of an egg, in a saucepan, stir in a heaping tablespoon of flour, add gradually to this a pint of rich milk, stirring constantly; take from the fire as it thickens. Butter a pudding dish, lay in a layer of noodles, then cheese, then sauce, then begin with noodles again until all is used up. Sprinkle cheese on top, a few cracker crumbs and flakes of butter here and there. Bake until brown.

NOODLES AND APPLES

Peel and cut six apples. Take broad noodles made out of three eggs, boil them fifteen minutes, drain, then mix with two tablespoons of fresh butter. Add some cinnamon and sugar to noodles. Put a layer of noodles, then apples and so on until pan is filled, being careful to have noodles on top. Put bits of fresh butter on top. Bake until apples are tender. If so desired, a milchig pie crust may be made and used as an under crust and when apples are tender and crust done, turn out on a large platter with crust side on top.

SCALLOPED NOODLES AND PRUNES

Make broad noodles with three eggs. Boil until tender, drain, pouring cold water through colander. Stew prunes, sprinkle with sugar and cinnamon. In a well-greased baking-dish place one-quarter of the noodles, bits of butter or other fat, add one-half of the prunes, then another layer of the noodles, butter or fat, the remaining prunes, the rest of the noodles. Pour over the prune juice and spread crumbs over top and bake in a moderate oven until crumbs are brown.

NOODLES AND MUSHROOMS

Make broad noodles, boil and serve with melted butter spread over the noodles and this sauce:

Brown a tablespoon of butter in the skillet, add one-half tablespoon of flour, then liquor of mushrooms, pinch of salt and pepper. When smooth, add mushrooms. Let boil and serve in a separate dish. When serving, a spoon of mushrooms is to be put over each portion of noodles.

GEROESTETE FERVELCHEN PFÄRVEL (EGG BARLEY)

Make just as you would a noodle dough, only stiffer, by adding and working in as much flour as possible and then grate on a coarse grater. Spread on a large platter to dry; boil one cup of egg barley in salt water or milk, which must boil before you put in the egg barley until thick. Serve with melted butter poured over them. (A simpler and much quicker way is to sift a cup or more of flour on a board; break in two eggs, and work the dough by rubbing it through your hands until it is as fine as barley grains.)

PFÄRVEL—FLEISCHIG

Make as much egg barley as required. Heat two tablespoons of fat, add one-quarter cup of onions, fry until golden brown, add the dried egg barley and brown nicely. Place in a pudding-dish, add three cups of hot soup stock or water to more than cover. Bake in a moderate oven about one hour or until the water has nearly all evaporated and the egg barley stands out like beads and is soft. The onion may be omitted. Serve hot in place of a vegetable.

KAESE KRAEPFLI (CHEESE KREPLICH)

Make a dough of one egg with a tablespoon of water; add a pinch of salt; work this just as you would noodle dough, quite stiff. Sift the flour in a bowl, break in the egg, add the salt and water, mix slowly by stirring with the handle of a knife, stirring in the same direction all the time. When this dough is so stiff that you cannot work it with the knife, flour your noodle board and work it with the hollow of your hands, always toward you, until the dough is perfectly smooth; roll out as thin as paper and cut into squares three inches in diameter. Fill with pot cheese or schmierkaese which has been prepared in the following manner: Stir up a piece of butter the size of an egg, adding one egg, sugar, cinnamon, grated peel of a lemon and pinch of salt, pounded almonds, which improve it; fill the kraepfli with a teaspoon, wet the edges with beaten egg, fold into triangles, pressing the edges firmly together; boil in boiling milk; when done they will swim to the top. Eat with melted butter or cream.

BOILED MACARONI

Break the macaroni into small pieces; boil for half an hour; drain and blanch in cold water. Reheat in tomato or cream sauce and serve. Grated cheese may be sprinkled over the dish if desired.

SPAGHETTI

Spaghetti is a small and more delicate form of macaroni. It is boiled until tender in salted water and is combined with cheese and with sauces the same as macaroni, and is usually left long. It makes a good garnish.

BAKED MACARONI WITH CHEESE

Cook one cup of broken macaroni in two quarts of boiling salted water for twenty or thirty minutes, drain and pour cold water through the colander. Put the macaroni in a pudding-dish in layers, covering each layer with cream sauce and grated cheese, one cup will be sufficient, and on the top layers sprinkle one cup of buttered bread crumbs. Bake in oven until the crumbs are brown.

SAVORY MACARONI

After baking; some flour to a pale fawn color pass it through a sieve or strainer to remove its gritty particles. Break half a pound of macaroni into short pieces, boil them in salted water until fairly tender, then drain.

In a little butter in a saucepan brown a level tablespoon of very finely chopped onion, then add three or four sliced tomatoes, a half teaspoon of powdered mixed herbs, a little nutmeg, salt and pepper. When the tomatoes are reduced to a pulp add one pint of milk and allow it to come to the boiling point before mixing with it two tablespoons of the browned flour moistened with water.

Stir and boil till smooth, press the whole through a strainer and return to the saucepan. When boiling, add the macaroni and a few minutes later stir in two tablespoons of grated or finely chopped cheese.

It may be served at once, but is vastly improved by keeping the pan for half an hour by the side of the fire in an outer vessel of water. Or the macaroni may be turned into a casserole and finished off in the oven.

For a meat meal the onions may be browned in sweet drippings or olive oil and soup stock substituted for the milk.

DUMPLINGS FOR STEW

Mix two teaspoons of baking powder with two cups of flour, one egg, one cup of cold water and a little salt.

Stir all lightly together and drop the batter from the spoon into the stew while the water continues to boil. Cover closely and do not uncover for twenty minutes, boiling constantly, but not too hard. Serve immediately in the stew.

SPAETZLEN OR SPATZEN

Sift two cups of flour into a bowl, make a depression in the centre and break into it two eggs, add a saltspoon of salt and enough water or milk to form a smooth, stiff dough. Set on some water to boil, salt the water and when the water boils drop the spaetzle into it, one at a time. Do this with the spoon with which you cut the dough, or roll it on a board into a round roll and cut them with a knife. When the spaetzle are done, they will rise to the surface, take them out with a perforated skimmer and lay them on a platter. Now heat two tablespoons of butter and add bread crumbs, let them brown for a minute and pour all over the spaetzle. If you prefer you may put the spaetzle right into the spider in which you have heated the butter. Another way to prepare them is after having taken them out of the water, heat some butter in a spider and put in the spaetzle, and then scramble a few eggs over all, stirring eggs and spaetzle together. Serve hot.

SOUR SPATZEN

Brown three tablespoons of flour with one tablespoon of sweet drippings, add a small onion finely chopped, then cover the spider and let the onion steam for a little while; do this over a low heat so there will be no danger of the union getting too brown; add vinegar and soup stock and two tablespoons of sugar. Let this boil until the sauce is of the right consistency. Serve with spaetzlen made according to the foregoing recipe, using water in place of the milk to form the dough. Pour the sauce over the spaetzlen before serving. By adding more sugar the sauce may be made sweet sour.

LEBERKNADEL (CALF LIVER DUMPLINGS)

Chop and pass through a colander one-half pound of calf's liver; rub to a cream four ounces of marrow, add the liver and stir hard. Then add a little thyme, one clove of garlic grated, pepper, salt and a little grated lemon peel, the yolks of two eggs and one whole egg. Then add enough grated bread crumbs or rolled crackers to this mixture to permit its being formed into little marbles. Drop in boiling salt water and let cook fifteen minutes; drain, roll in fine crumbs and fry in hot fat.

MILK OR POTATO NOODLES

Boil seven or eight potatoes, peel and let them stand several hours to dry; then grate them and add two eggs, salt and enough flour to make a dough thick enough to roll. Roll into long, round noodles as thick as two pencils and cut to length of baking-pan. Butter pan and lay noodles next to each other; cover with milk and lumps of butter and bake fifteen minutes, till yellow; serve immediately with bread crumbs browned in butter.

KARTOFFEL KLOESSE (POTATO DUMPLINGS)

Boil about eight potatoes in their jackets and when peeled lay them on a platter overnight. When ready to use them next day, grate, add two eggs, salt, a little nutmeg if desired, one wine-glass of farina, a tablespoon of chicken fat, one scant cup of flour gradually, and if not dry enough add more flour, but be sure not to make the mixture too stiff as this makes the balls heavy. Place balls in salted boiling water, cook until light and thoroughly done, serve just, as they are or fried in chicken fat until brown.

The dumplings may be made of the same mixture and in the centre of each dumpling place stripes of bread one inch long and one-fourth inch thick which have been fried in chicken fat and onions. Flour your hands well and make into dumplings. Put into boiling-salted water, boil about twenty-five minutes. Serve at once with chopped onions browned, or browned bread crumbs and chicken fat.

WIENER KARTOFFEL KLOESSE

Boil eight potatoes. When they are very soft drain off every drop of water, lay them on a clean baking-board and mash them while hot with a rolling-pin, adding about one cup of flour. When thoroughly mashed, break in two eggs, salt to taste, and flavor with grated nutmeg. Now flour the board thickly and foil out this potato dough about as thick as your little finger and spread with the following: Heat some fresh goose fat in a spider, cut up part of an onion very fine, add it to the hot fat together with one-half cup of grated bread crumbs. When brown, spread over the dough and roll just as you would a jelly-roll. Cut into desired lengths (about three or four inches), put them in boiling water, slightly salted, and boil uncovered for about fifteen minutes. Pour some hot goose grease over the dumplings.

BAIRISCHE DAMPFNUDELN, No. 1

Soak one cake of compressed yeast in a cup of lukewarm milk with a teaspoon of sugar, a teaspoon of salt, and sift a pint of flour in a bowl, in which you may also stir a small cup of milk and one egg. Pour in the yeast and work all thoroughly, adding more flour, but guarding against getting the dough too stiff. Cover up the bowl of dough and let it raise until it is as high again, which will take at least four hours. Flour a baking-board and mold small biscuits out of your dough, let them raise at least half an hour. Then butter a large, round, deep pan and set in your dumplings, brushing each with melted butter as you do so. When all are in, pour in enough milk to reach just half way up to the dumplings. Bake until a light brown. Eat hot, with vanilla sauce.

BAIRISCHE DAMPFNUDELN, No. 2

Make the dough just as you would in the above recipe, adding a tablespoon of butter, and after they have risen steam instead of baking them. If you have no steamer improvise one in this way: Put on a kettle of boiling water, set a colander on top of the kettle and lay in your dumplings, but do not crowd them; cover with a close-fitting lid and put a weight on top of it to keep in the steam, when done they will be as large again as when first put in. Take up one at first to try whether it is done by tearing open with two forks. If you have more than enough for your family, bake a pan of biscuits out of the remaining dough. Serve dumplings hot with prune sauce.

APPLE SLUMP

Pare, core and quarter apples, add a little water and sugar to taste, stew until tender and cover with the following mixture: Sift one pint of flour and one teaspoon of baking powder, add a pinch of salt and two cups of milk, mix and turn out onto a lightly floured board. Roll to one-half inch thickness and place over the stewed apples, cover and cook for ten minutes without lifting the lid. Serve hot with cream and sugar or soft custard.

BOILED APPLE DUMPLINGS

Beat well, without separating, two eggs, add a pinch of salt, two cups of milk and one cup of flour. To a second cup of flour, add two teaspoons of baking powder; add this to the batter and as much more flour as is necessary to make a soft dough. Roll out quickly one-half inch thick. Cut into squares, lay two or three quarters of pared apples on each, sprinkle with sugar and pinch the dough around the apples. Have a number of pudding cloths ready, wrung out of cold water, and sprinkle well with flour. Put a dumpling in each, leave a little room for swelling and tie tightly. Drop into a kettle of rapidly boiling water and keep the water at a steady boil for an hour. Serve hot with hard sauce.

Have a saucer in the bottom of kettle to prevent burning.

FARINA DUMPLINGS

Beat yolks of four eggs with three tablespoons of goose, turkey or chicken fat, but if these are not convenient, clear beef drippings will do. Put in enough farina to make a good Batter. Beat whites of eggs to a stiff froth with pinch of salt, and stir in batter. Put on in large boiler sufficient water to boil dumplings and add one tablespoon of salt. When boiling drop in by tablespoons. Boil one hour. This quantity makes twenty dumplings.

HUCKLEBERRY DUMPLINGS

Take a loaf of stale bread; cut off the crust and soak in cold water, then squeeze dry. Beat three eggs light, yolks and whites together add one quart berries and mix all together with a little brown sugar and a pinch of salt. Boil steadily one hour, serve with hard sauce.

PLUM KNOEDEL (HUNGARIAN)

Boil several potatoes, mash, mix with one egg yolk, a little salt and enough flour to make a dough soft enough to hold the impress of the finger. Roll out and cut into four-cornered pieces; in each square place a German plum which has had the pits removed and a mixture of sugar and cinnamon; put in place of the pit. Roll each square into a round dumpling; put these into a pan with boiling; salted water and let them cook covered for six or eight minutes. When done, serve with some bread crumbs browned in butter or schmalz and spread over the knoedel.

PEAR DUMPLING (BIRNE KLOESSE)

Take half a loaf of white bread or as much stale white bread, soak the white part and grate the crust, add one cup of suet chopped very fine, one cup of flour, one egg, salt and spices to taste, and one-half teaspoon of baking-powder. Make this into a dumpling, put it on a tiny plate in a large kettle. Lay prunes and pears around, about a pound of each, one cup of brown sugar, two pieces of stick cinnamon, dash of claret and cold water to almost cover; then cover kettle tightly and boil four hours. Serve hot.

Prunes and dried apples may be used as well.

PEACH DUMPLINGS

Make a dough of a quart of flour and a pint of milk, or water, a tablespoon of shortening, a pinch of salt, one egg and a spoon of sugar; add a piece of compressed yeast, which has previously been dissolved in water. Let the dough raise for three hours. In the meantime make a compote of peaches by stewing them with sugar and spices, such as cinnamon and cloves. Stew enough to answer for both sauce and filling. When raised, flour the baking-board and roll out the dough half an inch thick. Cut cakes out of it with a tumbler, brush the edges with white of egg, put a teaspoon of peach compote in the centre of a cake and cover it with another layer of cake and press the edges firmly together. Steam over boiling water and serve with peach sauce. A delicious dessert may also be made by letting the dough rise another half hour after being rolled out, and before cutting.

Compote of huckleberries may be used with these dumplings instead of peaches, if so desired.

CHERRY ROLEY-POLEY

Make a rich baking-powder biscuit dough, and roll it out until it is about two-thirds of an inch thick. Pit and stew enough cherries to make a thick layer of fruit and add sugar to taste. Spread them over the dough thickly and roll it up, taking care to keep the cherries from falling out. Wrap a cloth around it, and sew it up loosely with coarse thread, which is easily pulled out. Allow plenty of room for the dough to rise. Lay the roley-poley on a plate, set it in a steamer and steam for an hour and a half. Serve in slices, with cream or sauce.

SHABBAS KUGEL

Soak five wheat rolls in water, then press the bread quite dry, add one cup of drippings or one-half pound of suet chopped very fine, a pinch of salt, two eggs well beaten, one teaspoon of cinnamon, one grated lemon rind, one-half cup of sugar, one tablespoon of water. Stir all together thoroughly, grease the kugel pot well with warm melted fat, pour in the mixture and send it Friday afternoon to the bakery where it will remain till Saturday noon; it will then be baked brown. If one has a coal range that will retain the heat for the length of time required, it will be baked nicely. The kugel must be warm, however, when served.

KUGEL (SCHARFE)

If one desires an unsweetened kugel omit the sugar and cinnamon in the recipe above and season with salt and pepper. When required for any other meal but Shabbas, a kugel can be baked brown in two hours.

SWEET POTATO PUDDING

Take one quart of grated, raw sweet potatoes, one tablespoon leach of meat fat and chicken fat, one half pound of brown sugar, one-half pint of molasses, one and one-half pints of cold water, one saltspoon of salt and a little black pepper, grated orange peel, ginger, nutmeg and cinnamon to taste. Pour into greased baking-pan and bake until it jellies. Bake in moderate oven. May be eaten as a dessert, warm or cold.

APPLE STRUDEL, No. 1

Sift two cups of flour, add pinch of salt and one teaspoon of powdered sugar. Stir in slowly one cup of lukewarm water, and work until dough does not stick to the hands. Flour board, and roll, as thin as possible. Do not tear. Place a tablecloth on table, put the rolled out dough on it, and pull gently with the hands, to get the dough as thin as tissue paper.

Have ready six apples chopped fine, and mixed with cinnamon, sugar, one-half cup of seedless raisins, one-half cup of currants. Spread this over the dough with plenty of chicken-fat or oil all over the apples. Take the tablecloth in both hands, and roll the strudel, over and over, holding the cloth high, and the strudel will almost roll itself. Grease a baking-pan, hold to the edge of the cloth, and roll the strudel in. Bake brown, basting often with fat or oil.

APPLE STRUDEL, No. 2

Into a large mixing bowl place one and one-half cups of flour and one-quarter teaspoon of salt. Beat one egg lightly and add it to one-third cup of warm water and combine the two mixtures. Mix the dough quickly with a knife; then knead it, place on board, stretching it up and down to make it elastic, until it leaves the board clean. Now toss it on a well-floured board, cover with a hot bowl and keep in a warm place. While preparing the filling lay the dough in the centre of a well-floured tablecloth on the table; roll out a little, brush well with some melted butter, and with hands under dough, palms down, pull and stretch the dough gently, until it is as large as the table and thin as paper, and do not tear the dough. Spread one quart of sour apples, peeled and cut fine, one-quarter pound of almonds blanched and chopped, one-half cup of raisins and currants, one cup of sugar and one teaspoon of cinnamon, evenly over three-quarters of the dough, and drop over them a few tablespoons of melted butter. Trim edges. Roll the dough over apples on one side, then hold cloth high with both hands and the strudel will roll itself over and over into one big roll, trim edges again. Then twist the roll to fit the greased pan. Bake in a hot oven until brown and crisp and brush with melted butter. If juicy small fruits or berries are used, sprinkle bread crumbs over the stretched dough to absorb the juices. Serve slightly warm.

RAHM STRUDEL

Prepare the dough as for Apple Strudel as directed in the foregoing recipe, drip one quart of thick sour milk on it lightly, with a large spoon, put one cup of grated bread crumbs over the milk, add two cups of granulated sugar, one cup of chopped almonds, one cup of raisins, and one teaspoon of cinnamon, roll and place in well-buttered pan, put small pieces of butter over the top, basting frequently. Serve warm with vanilla sauce. One-half this quantity may be used for a small strudel.

CHERRY STRUDEL

Make a dough of two cups of flour, a pinch of salt and a little lukewarm water; do not make it too stiff, but smooth. Slap the dough back and forth. Do this repeatedly for about fifteen minutes. Now put the dough in a warm, covered bowl and set it in a warm, place for half an hour. In the meantime stem and pit two quarts of sour cherries. Grate into them some stale bread (about a plateful); also the peel of half a lemon, and mix. Add one cup of sugar, some ground cinnamon and about four ounces of pounded sweet almonds, mix all thoroughly. Roll out the dough as thin as possible, lay aside the rolling-pin and pull, or rather stretch the dough as thin as tissue paper. In doing this you will have to walk all around the table, for when well stretched it will cover more than the size of an ordinary table. Pull off all of the thick edge, for it must be very thin to be good (save the pieces for another strudel). Pour a little melted goose-oil or butter over this, and sprinkle the bread, sugar, almonds, cherries, etc., over it; roll the strudel together into a long roll. Have ready a long baking-pan well greased with either butter or goose-fat; fold the strudel into the shape of a pretzel. Butter or grease top also and bake a light brown; baste often while baking. Eat warm.

MANDEL (ALMOND) STRUDEL

Prepare the dough as for Apple Strudel No. 2. Blanch one-half pound of almonds and grind, when dried beat the yolks of four eggs light with one-quarter pound of granulated sugar, add the grated peel of one lemon and mix in the almonds. Spread over the dough with plenty of oil, butter or fat and roll. Bake; baste very often.

CABBAGE STRUDEL

Heat one-half cup of goose-fat, add one medium-sized cabbage and let it simmer until done, stirring constantly to keep from burning. While cooling prepare strudel dough, fill with cabbage and one cup of raisins and currants mixed, two cups of granulated sugar, one-half cup of chopped almonds and one teaspoon cinnamon, roll and put little pieces of grease on top; bake in hot oven and baste frequently. The pans in which the strudel is baked must be greased generously. Serve this strudel hot. This strudel may be made for a milk meal by substituting butter for fat.

QUARK STRUDEL (DUTCH CHEESE)

Make a strudel or roley-poley dough and let it rest until you have prepared the cheese. Take half a pound of cheese, rub it through a coarse sieve or colander, add salt, the yolks of two eggs and one whole egg, sweeten to taste. Add the grated peel of one lemon, two ounces of sweet almonds, and about four bitter ones, blanched and pounded, four ounces of sultana raisins and a little citron chopped fine. Now roll out as thin as possible, spread in the cheese, roll and bake, basting with sweet cream.

STRUDEL AUS KALBSLUNGE

Wash the lung and heart thoroughly in salt water, and put on to boil in cold water, adding salt, one onion, a few bay leaves and cook until very tender. Make the dough precisely the same as any other strudel. Take the boiled lung and heart, chop them as fine as possible and stew in a saucepan with some fat, adding chopped parsley, a little salt, pepper and mace, or nutmeg, the grated peel of half a lemon and a little wine. Add the beaten yolks of two eggs to thicken, and remove from the fire to cool. Roll out the dough as thin as possible, fill in the mixture and lay the strudel in a well-greased pan; put flakes of fat on top and baste often. Eat hot.

RICE STRUDEL

Prepare the dough same as for Apple Strudel. Leave it in a warm place covered, until you have prepared the rice. Wash a quarter of a pound of rice in hot water—about three times—then boil it in milk until very soft and thick. Let it cool, and then add two ounces of butter, the yolks of four eggs, four ounces of sugar and one teaspoon of vanilla, some salt and the beaten whites of two eggs, mix thoroughly. When your dough has been rolled out and pulled as thin as possible, spread the rice over it and roll. Add pounded almonds and raisins if desired. Put in a greased pan and bake until brown, basting with sweet cream or butter.

CEREALS

The cereals are the most valuable of the vegetable foods, including as they do the grains from which is made nearly all the bread of the world.

For family use, cereals should be bought in small quantities and kept in glass jars, tightly covered.

Variety is to be found in using the different cereals and preparing them in new ways. Many cereals are improved by adding a little milk during the latter part of the cooking. Boiling water and salt should always be added to cereals, one teaspoon salt to one cup of cereal. Long cooking improves the flavor and makes the cereal more digestible.

Cereals should be cooked the first five minutes over the fire and then over hot-water in a double boiler; if one cannot be procured, cook cereal in a saucepan set in a larger one holding the hot water.

LAWS ABOUT CEREALS

To discover if cereals such as barley, wheat, oats, farina or cornmeal are kosher, place them on a hot plate, if no worms or other insects appear they are fit to be eaten, if not, they must be thrown away.

If flour is mildewed it must be destroyed.

OATMEAL PORRIDGE

As oatmeal is ground in different grades of coarseness, the time for cooking varies and it is best to follow the directions given on the packages. The meal should be cooked until soft, but should not be mushy. The ordinary rule is to put a cup of meal into two cups of salted boiling water (a teaspoon of salt), and let it cook in a double boiler the required time. Keep covered until done; then remove the cover and let the moisture escape.

COLD OATMEAL

Oatmeal is very good cold, and in summer is better served in that way. It can be turned into fancy molds or into small cups to cool, and will then hold the form and make an ornamental dish.

OATMEAL WITH CHEESE

Cook one cup of oatmeal overnight and just before serving add one tablespoon of butter and one cup grated cheese. Stir until the cheese is melted and serve at once.

BAKED APPLE WITH OATMEAL

Pare and core the apples and fill the core space with left-over oatmeal mush. Put the apples in a baking dish; sprinkle with sugar; pour a little water into the bottom of the pan and bake in a moderate oven until the apples are tender. Serve warm with cream for breakfast or luncheon.

WHEAT CEREALS

Wheat cereals, like oatmeal, are best cooked by following the directions on the package. Most of them are greatly improved by the addition of a little milk or by a few chopped dates or whole sultana raisins.

CORNMEAL MUSH

Mix together one cup of cornmeal and one teaspoon of salt, and add one cup of cold water gradually, stirring until smooth. Pour this mixture into two cups of boiling; water in a double boiler and cook from three to five hours. Serve hot with cream and sugar.

SAUTÉD CORNMEAL MUSH

Put left-over mush into a dish and smooth it over the top. When cold cut into slices one-half inch thick. Dip each slice into flour. Melt one-half teaspoon of drippings in a frying-pan and be careful to let it get smoking hot. Brown the floured slices on each side. Drain if necessary and serve on a hot plate with syrup.

FARINA

To one-half cup of farina take one teaspoon of salt; pour gradually into three cups of boiling water and cook the mixture in a double boiler for about one hour.

HOMINY

Get the unbroken hominy and after careful washing soak it twenty-four hours in the water. Cook one cup of hominy slowly in the same water in a covered vessel for eight hours or until all the water has been absorbed by the hominy; add two tablespoons of butter, one teaspoon of salt and two tablespoons of cream and serve as a vegetable or as a cereal with sugar and cream.

MARMELITTA

Take two cups of coarse cornmeal and four cups of cold water put on to boil; add one-half teaspoon of salt. Stir the cornmeal continually and when done place on platter, spread with butter, sharf cheese or any cheese such as pot or cream cheese. To be eaten warm.

POLENTA

Place one cup of yellow cornmeal and three cups of cold water in a double boiler, add one teaspoon of salt, one-half teaspoon of pepper and cook for forty minutes. While still hot add one and one-half cups of grated cheese to the mixture and heat until it melts. Turn the mixture into a greased bowl and allow it to set. The meal may be sliced an inch thick or cut with a biscuit cutter and then fried in hot vegetable oil. Serve with white or tomato sauce as desired.

BARLEY, TAPIOCA, SAGO, ETC

Add one teaspoon of salt to one quart of boiling water and pour gradually on one-half cup of barley or other hard grain and boil until tender, from one to two or more hours, according to the grain, and have each kernel stand out distinct when done. Add more boiling water as it evaporates. Use as a vegetable or in soups. Pearl barley, tapioca and sago cook quicker than other large grains.

BOILED RICE

Put one-half cup of rice in a strainer; place the strainer over a bowl nearly full of cold water; rub the rice; lift the strainer from the bowl and change the water. Repeat this until the water in the bowl is clear. Have two quarts of water boiling briskly, add the rice and one tablespoon of salt gradually so as not to stop the boiling; boil twenty minutes or until soft, do not stir; drain through a colander and place the colander over boiling water for ten minutes to steam. Every grain will be distinct. Serve as a vegetable or as a cereal with cream and sugar.

RICE IN MILK

Clean the rice as for boiling in water; and cook one-half cup of rice with one and one-half cups of hot milk and one-half teaspoon of salt, adding a few seeded or sultana raisins if desired. Serve hot like boiled rice or press into small cups, cool and serve with cream and sugar.

RICE WITH GRATED CHOCOLATE

Cook one-half cup of rice, place in hot serving dish, sprinkle generously with grated sweet chocolate; set in oven one minute and serve.

STEAMED RICE

Wash two cups of rice carefully put in double boiler; add eight cups of cold water and a pinch of salt and steam for two hours; do not stir. Serve with any kind of stewed fruit or preserve.

APPLES WITH RICE

Boil one cup of rice in water or milk; rub the kettle all over with a piece of butter before putting in the rice, season with salt and add a lump of butter. When cooked, add about six apples, pared, quartered and cored, sugar and cinnamon. This makes a nice side dish, or dessert, served with cream.

BOILED RICE WITH PINEAPPLE

Boil as much rice as desired and when done slice up the pineapple and add, with as much sugar as is required to sweeten to taste.

BAKED RICE

Arrange two cups of boiled rice in a baking dish in layers, covering each with grated cheese, a little milk, butter, salt and red pepper. Spread one cup of grated bread crumbs over all and bake in a moderate oven until the crumbs are browned.

SWEET RICE

Clean and wash one cup of rice. Put on to boil with cold water, add a pinch of salt. When done drain off the water, if any; add two cups of milk, stir in and let boil for five minutes. Dish up, then sprinkle sugar and cinnamon generously over the top. The yolk of an egg can be added just before serving if desired.

EGGS BAKED IN RICE

Line a buttered dish with steamed rice. Break the eggs in the centre, dot with butter, sprinkle with salt, pepper and bake in a moderate oven.

RICE AND NUT LOAF

Boil one-half cup of rice (brown preferred); drain and dry it. Mix with an equal quantity of bread crumbs. Add level teaspoon of salt and one-half saltspoon of black pepper. Stir in one cup of chopped nuts—pecans or peanuts. Add one tablespoon of chopped parsley and one egg. Mix thoroughly and pack in bread-pan to mold it. Turn it from pan into baking-pan and bake slowly three-quarters of an hour. Serve with cream sauce or purée of peas.

PILAF

Put two cups of water on to boil, add juice of two tomatoes and a pinch of salt. When boiling, add one cup of rice and let cook until the water has evaporated. Then add melted butter, mix well, and keep in warm place, covered, until ready to serve.

SPANISH RICE

Put one cup of washed rice in frying-pan with four or five tablespoons of poultry fat; add three onions chopped and two cloves of garlic minced fine. Fry ten minutes; add one red pepper or one canned pimento chopped, or one teaspoon of paprika, and three ripe tomatoes or two cups of strained tomatoes and one teaspoon of salt. Cook slowly about one hour, and as the water evaporates, add more boiling water to keep from burning.

LEFT-OVER CEREALS

Oatmeal, hominy, cracked wheat, and other cereals which are left over can be added next day to the fresh stock, for they are improved by long boiling and do not injure the new supply, or such as is left can be molded in large or in small forms, and served cold with cream, or milk and sugar. In warm weather cereals are nicer cold than hot. Cold hominy and mush, cut into squares and fried, so that a crisp crust is formed on both sides,—also hominy or farina, rolled into balls and fried,—are good used in place of a vegetable or as a breakfast dish.

Any of the cereals make good pancakes, or a small amount added to the ordinary pancake batter improves it.

EGGS

Eggs and the foods into which they enter are favorite articles of diet in most households. They are an agreeable substitute for meat and even when high in price make a cheaper dish than meat.

A fresh egg should feel heavy, sink in water, and when held to a bright light show a clear round yolk.

TO PRESERVE EGGS

In the early spring or fall when eggs are plentiful and at their best, pack them away for future use. Use strictly fresh eggs with perfect shells (no cracks). Buy water glass at drugstore. Use ten parts water to one of water glass. Boil water, when cool add water glass and beat well. Use an earthen jar or crock, pack in rows and pour over the liquid mixture to cover well. Place old plate over eggs in crock to keep them under water. Put cover on jar and keep in cool place. More eggs may be added at any time if well covered with the liquid mixture.

For fifteen dozen eggs use one quart water glass.

TO KEEP EGG YOLKS

The yolks may be kept several days and be as if just separated from the whites if they are placed in a cup previously rinsed with cold water and a pinch of salt added to them. The cup must be closely covered with a wet cloth, and this must be changed and well rinsed in cold water every day.

When whites are left over make a small angel cake or any of the cookies which require the whites of egg only.

When yolks are left over use for making mayonnaise.

POACHED OR DROPPED EGGS

Fill a pan with boiling, salted water. Break each egg into a wet saucer and slip it into the water; set the pan back where water will not boil. Dip the water over the eggs with a spoon. When the white is firm and a film has formed over the yolk, they are cooked. Take them up with a skimmer, drain and serve hot, on toast. Season with salt.

BOILED EGGS

Soft-boiled eggs may be prepared in two ways. The eggs may be dropped carefully into boiling water and boiled three minutes, or they may be placed in a covered vessel of boiling water and allowed to stand in a warm place (but not on the stove) for ten minutes. Eggs prepared in this way are sometimes called "Coddled Eggs." They are much more delicate and digestible than the usual "Boiled Eggs."

Hard-boiled eggs should be cooked in boiling water for fifteen or twenty minutes and then dropped in cold water to prevent the yolk from turning dark.

SCRAMBLED EGGS

Break into a bowl as many eggs as required, add salt and pepper. Have some very hot butter in the frying-pan on the stove; pour in the eggs, stir constantly until set, not stiff, and serve on a hot platter at once.

FRIED EGGS

Melt in a frying-pan a piece of butter, or fat for a meat meal. When hot, drop in the eggs, one at a time, being careful not to break the yolk. When the white of the egg is set they are done, though some persons like them turned over and cooked on the other side. Remove from the pan with a cake turner.

BAKED EGGS

Butter individual baking dishes and break an egg in each, being careful to keep the yolk whole. Put on each egg a bit of butter, a little pepper and salt. Bake in moderate oven from four to six minutes.

BAKED EGGS WITH CHEESE

Butter a baking dish of a size necessary for number of eggs desired, break eggs into dish, add salt, paprika, pepper to taste, one tablespoon of cream, and two tablespoons of grated cheese.

Place dish in a pan of hot water in moderate oven for five minutes until eggs are set.

TOMATO WITH EGG

Cut top from tomatoes, remove seeds, put a raw egg in each tomato, dust with salt, pepper, and finely chopped parsley. Place in moderate oven until egg is set. Serve with cream sauce.

BAKED EGG WITH TOMATOES

Remove the skin from six fresh tomatoes or take one-half can of tomatoes, chop them and put them on stove and cook for twenty minutes; season with one tablespoon of chopped parsley, half an onion chopped, salt and pepper; thicken at the end of that time with one teaspoon of melted butter mixed with one tablespoon of flour. Put aside to cool. Then mix in the yolks of four eggs well beaten, and lastly cut and fold in the four whites. Butter a pudding dish and set this mixture in the oven in a pan of lukewarm water and bake in a moderate oven until a golden brown.

PLAIN OMELET

To make an omelet for breakfast or luncheon for two persons, take three eggs, three tablespoons of sweet milk and a saltspoon of salt. Whip the yolks of the eggs, the milk and salt to a light foam with an egg whip. Slowly add the yolk mixture to the whites of the eggs, which should be beaten to a stiff froth in a big bowl. After the yolks and milk are well whipped through the whites, beat the whole together for a few minutes with the egg-beater.

In an omelet pan or a large frying-pan put a tablespoon of good butter. When the butter is bubbling hot, pour in the omelet mixture. Stir it lightly for the first minute with a broad-bladed knife, then stop stirring it; and, as the mixture begins to stiffen around the edge, fold the omelet toward the centre with the knife. As soon as it is properly folded, turn it over on a hot platter. Decorate with sprigs of parsley and serve.

SWEET OMELET

Six eggs, two tablespoons of flour, one cup of cold milk. Wet the flour with a little of the milk, then add the rest of the milk and the yolks of the eggs. Beat the whites of the eggs to a stiff froth and pour into the flour, milk and yolks. Put a piece of butter into a spider and let it get hot, but not so hot that the butter will burn. Then pour the mixture in and put in a moderate oven to bake in the spider. It takes about ten minutes to bake. Then slip a knife under it and loosen it and slip off on a large plate. Sift powdered sugar on top and serve with a slice of lemon.

SWEET OMELET FOR ONE

One egg, beat white separately, two tablespoons of cold sweet milk, a pinch of salt. Brown on both sides or roll, spread with compote or sprinkle powdered sugar thickly over it. Serve at once.

SPANISH OMELET

In a chopping bowl place two nice large ripe tomatoes, first peeling them; one large or two medium-sized white Texas onions, two sprigs of parsley, and one large green-bell pepper, first removing most of its seeds.

Chop these ingredients well together quite fine, turn them into a saucepan and let them cook over rather a brisk heat until quite soft. Put no water in this mixture. Add a tablespoon of olive oil or of butter before it begins to cook and season well with salt and red pepper.

Make the omelet the same as the plain one, but use water instead of milk in mixing it, and only use two tablespoons of water for the six eggs required.

After the eggs are sufficiently beaten, mixed, and in the pan over the fire, and when the edges begin to stiffen, cover the surface of the omelet to within an inch of the edge with the cooked vegetables. Fold the omelet quickly and turn it on a hot platter. Pour around it all the vegetables left in the pan and serve.

RUM OMELET

Take six eggs, beat whites and yolks well, add a pinch of salt and a teaspoon of brandy. Fry in a spider quickly and spread with a compote of huckleberries or any other fruit. Roll up the omelet, pour a very small wineglass of rum over it, light it and serve at once.

SWEET ALMOND OMELET

Prepare one-half cup of sweet almonds, blanched, chopped fine and pounded smooth. Beat four eggs slightly, add four tablespoons of cream and turn it into a hot omelet pan on which you have melted one tablespoon, of butter. Cook carefully, drawing the cooked portion into the centre and tilting the pan to allow the liquid part to run over the bare pan. When nearly all set, sprinkle the almonds over the surface and turn the edges over until well rolled. Then slip it out on a hot dish and dredge with powdered sugar, and scatter several salted almonds over the top. Serve immediately.

CORN OMELET

Take one-half cup of canned corn and chop it very fine (or the same amount cut from the cob). Add to that the yolk of one egg, well beaten with pepper and salt to taste, and two tablespoons of cream. Beat the white of the egg very stiff and stir in just before cooking. Have the pan very hot and profusely buttered. Pour the mixture on, and when nicely browned, turn one half over the other, as in cooking other omelets.

HERB OMELET

Take six eggs and beat well in a bowl. Add two tablespoons of cold water and a quarter of a teaspoon of salt, a pinch of pepper, a teaspoon of chopped parsley, a quarter of a teaspoon of grated onion and a teaspoon of fine butter, shaved in little pieces. Mix well with a wooden spoon. Dissolve in the spider the butter and add at once the beaten eggs, etc., inclining the spider to the handle for an instant and then shaking the omelet into the centre and turn up the right edge, then the left and fry briskly five minutes and serve.

POACHED EGGS WITH FRIED TOMATOES

Fry tomatoes (cut one-half inch thick) in butter, pepper and salt. Have prepared slices of bread cut round, and fried in butter. Put on a hot platter with a slice of tomato on each. Poach as many eggs as are required, in boiling salt water. Lift out very carefully, placing one egg on each tomato. Add to the gravy in which tomatoes were fried, two tablespoons of cream, one teaspoon of any pungent sauce, one teaspoon of mushroom catsup, juice of half a lemon, and a teaspoon of flour to thicken. Cook up once and pour over eggs. Serve very hot.

EGGS POACHED IN TOMATO SAUCE

Make a sauce of one tablespoon of butter, one tablespoon of flour, one and one-half cups of canned tomatoes rubbed through a strainer, a pinch of soda, salt, pepper and sugar to taste. When sufficiently cooked drop in the required number of eggs, cook until the white is firm, basting the eggs often with the sauce. When done, lift the eggs carefully to squares of toast and pour the sauce around them.

EGGS PIQUANT

Set to boil the following mixture: Pour into the kettle water to the depth of about one inch, adding a little salt and half a cup of vinegar. When this boils, break in as many fresh eggs, one at a time, as you desire to have. Do this carefully so as not to break the yolks. As soon as the whites of the eggs are boiled, take up carefully with a perforated skimmer and lay in cold water. Then remove to a large platter and pour over the following sauce: Strain the sauce the eggs were boiled in and set away until you have rubbed or grated two hard-boiled eggs, yolks only. Add a tablespoon of butter rubbed very hard and add also some sugar and part of the strained sauce. Boil up once and pour over the eggs. Garnish with parsley.

OMELET SOUFFLÉ

Yolks of six eggs and six tablespoons of powdered sugar, added gradually, and both beaten together until thick and smooth; juice of one lemon and a little grated rind; whites beaten as stiff as possible, stirred together. Put into a warm well-buttered dish; bake in quick oven ten minutes.

WHITE SAUCE OMELET

Make a white sauce of one tablespoon of butter blended with two tablespoons of flour, one-half teaspoon of salt, pinch of pepper and one teaspoon of sugar, adding one-half cup each of milk and cream. Beat the yolks of five eggs and stir them into the sauce, then add the stiffly beaten whites of the eggs, folding them in carefully. Melt two tablespoons of butter in the omelet pan, when it is hot put in the mixture and let it stand in a moderate heat for two minutes, place in a hot oven and cook until set. Remove from the oven, turn on a hot platter and serve.

EGGS WITH CREAM DRESSING

Blend two tablespoons of butter with three tablespoons of flour. Place on range and stir until the butter is melted. Add one and one-half cups of milk, stirring all the time until the mixture is thick; season with one teaspoon of salt and a few grains of pepper. Separate the whites of six hard-boiled eggs from the yolks. Chop the whites fine and add to the dressing. Arrange slices of toast on a hot platter, pour the dressing over them; force the yolks through a ricer onto the toast and dressing; serve hot.

SCALLOPED EGGS

Use above recipe and mix one cup of bread crumbs with one tablespoon of butter, sprinkle this over dish and bake fifteen minutes in a hot oven.

EGGS À LA MEXICANA

Boil six dried Spanish peppers twenty minutes. Drain, remove the seeds, and chop fine. Fry in butter half an onion and one clove of garlic. Add one cup of uncooked rice, cover with one cup of water and cook till tender. Add a lump of butter, salt, and, when done, cover with six eggs; then scramble all together. Serve on a hot dish.

EGGS SPANISH

Boil eggs hard; after cooling, remove shells and halve lengthwise. Cook for thirty minutes fresh or canned tomatoes with minced green onions, garlic, parsley, a laurel leaf, salt, pepper, and cayenne pepper to taste. Strain. Melt a slice of butter, add a little flour, and then add sauce gradually. Cook ten minutes; place eggs carefully in sauce and serve.

FRESH MUSHROOMS WITH EGGS

Peel nine good-sized mushrooms without using the stems and chop very fine; fry two tablespoons of butter and two finely chopped onions without browning. Add the mushrooms and steam them by covering the pan after seasoning with salt, pepper and paprika. Before serving, beat six whole eggs and scramble with the mushrooms. Serve on hot buttered toast.

EGG RAREBIT

Make a cream sauce. Grate one-half pound American and Swiss cheese mixed, or American alone; add to the sauce. Chop three hard-boiled eggs, add to the sauce, season with salt and pepper, and serve on buttered toast.

KROSPHADA

Place two sliced onions with two ounces each of sugar and spices, pepper and salt to taste, in a pint of pure malt vinegar and boil gently until the onions are nearly done. Let it cool a little and then stir in six beaten eggs and sufficient crumbled ginger-bread to make the whole quite thick. Place again over the fire for a few minutes, stirring frequently and mashing the mixture into a uniform paste, but be very careful that it does not boil.

CURRIED EGGS

Melt four tablespoons of butter in a frying-pan, add one onion chopped fine and cook until straw colored. Then add one tablespoon of curry powder. Make a smooth paste of one-fourth of a cup of water and two tablespoons of flour; add one tablespoon of lemon juice and one-half teaspoon of salt. Add to the first mixture; boil five minutes. Arrange six hard-boiled eggs in a border of rice and pour the dressing over all.

FRICASSEED EGGS

Take six hard-boiled eggs, remove shells. Roll them in flour, then in egg to which has been added one-half teaspoon of oil, one-half teaspoon of vinegar, a few drops of onion juice, one teaspoon chopped parsley, a little nutmeg and salt. When quite covered, roll in vermicelli that has been broken into fine bits and fry in deep beef drippings. Serve with the following sauce: One tablespoon of fat; one tablespoon of flour, browned together; add one-half cup of white wine and a cup of bouillon. Season with salt and cayenne and boil five minutes. Add one teaspoon each of chopped chives and parsley, some chopped olives and mushrooms; bring to a boil again and pour over the eggs.

EGGS EN MARINADE

Mix equal quantities of water and good meat gravy, two tablespoons each, with a teaspoon of vinegar and a seasoning of pepper and salt. Put in a stew-pan and stir in gradually two well-beaten, yolks of eggs. When it thickens and before it boils, have ready a half dozen nicely poached eggs and pour the sauce over them. Garnish with parsley.

SCALLOPED EGGS (FLEISCHIG)

Make a force-meat of chopped tongue, bread crumbs, pepper, salt, a little parsley, one tablespoon of melted fat, and soup stock enough to make a soft paste. Half fill patty-pans with the mixture. Break an egg carefully on the top of each, sprinkle with a little salt, pepper and cracker dust. Put in the oven and bake about ten minutes. Serve hot.

SCRAMBLED EGGS WITH BRAINS

Scald brains with hot water, clean and skin, and boil a few minutes in fresh water. Melt a little fat in skillet, put in brains, finely chopped, and stir well until dry and done. Add one teaspoon of chopped parsley, pinch of salt, and three eggs well-beaten. Stir with a fork until eggs are evenly cooked, put on hot platter, and serve immediately.

SCRAMBLED EGGS WITH SAUSAGE

Take one pound of cold, boiled sausage, skin and slice in half-inch pieces. Place in a frying-pan with two tablespoons of hot fat; brown on both sides a few minutes and just before serving add three eggs, beaten slightly; mix; and cook until the eggs are set and serve immediately.

Chopped tongue root may be used instead of sausage.

SMOKED BRISKET OF BEEF AND EGGS

Take slices of smoked breast of beef, brown in frying-pan; place on hot platter. Slip as many eggs as are needed in frying-pan and cook gently by dripping the hot fat over them until done. Place carefully on the beef slices and serve at once.

CHEESE

Cheese should not be tightly covered. When it becomes dry and hard, grate and keep covered until ready to use. It may be added to starchy foods.

Care should be exercised in planning meals in which cheese is employed as a substitute for meat. As cheese dishes are inclined to be somewhat "heavy," they should be offset by crisp, watery vegetables, water cress, celery, lettuce, fruit salads and light desserts, preferably fresh or cooked fruit. Another point, too, is to be considered. Whether raw or cooked, cheese seems to call for the harder kinds of bread—crusty rolls or biscuits, zwieback, toast, pulled bread or hard crackers.

A soft, crumbly cheese is best for cooking.

Cheese is sufficiently cooked when melted, if cooked longer it becomes tough and leathery.

Baking-soda in cheese dishes which are cooked makes the casein more digestible.

COTTAGE CHEESE (POT CHEESE)

Heat sour milk slowly until the whey rises to the top; pour it off, put the curd in a bag and let it dry for six hours without squeezing it. Pour it into a bowl and break it fine with a wooden spoon. Season with salt. Mold into balls and keep in a cool place. It is best when fresh.

KOCH KAESE (BOILED CHEESE)

Press one quart of fine cottage cheese through a coarse sieve or colander and set it away in a cool place for a week, stirring it once or twice during that time; when it has become quite strong, stir it smooth with a wooden or silver spoon; add a saltspoon of salt and one-fourth as much of caraway seed, yolks of two eggs and an even tablespoon of flour which has been previously dissolved in about one-half cup of cold milk; stir the flour and milk until it is a smooth paste, adding a lump of butter, about the size of an egg; add all to the cheese. Put the cheese on to boil until quite thick; stirring occasionally; boil altogether about one-half hour, stirring constantly the last ten minutes; the cheese must look smooth as velvet. Pour it into a dish which has been previously rinsed in cold water. Set it away in a cool place; to keep it any length of time, cover it with a clean cloth which has been dipped in and wrung out of beer. This cheese is excellent for rye bread sandwiches.

A DELICIOUS CREAM CHEESE

Sweet milk is allowed to stand until it is like a jelly, but does not separate. Then it is poured into a cheese-cloth bag and hung up to drain until all the water is out of it and only the rich creamy substance remains. Sometimes it takes from twelve to twenty-four hours. At the end of this time the cheese is turned from the bag into a bowl; then to every pint of the cheesy substance a tablespoon of butter is added and enough salt to season it palatably. Then it is whipped up with a fork until it is a smooth paste and enough put on a plate to make a little brick, like a Philadelphia cheese. With two knives, one in each hand, lightly press the cheese together in the shape of a brick, smooth it over the top and put it away to cool. One quart of rich sour milk will make a good sized cheese.

CHEESE BALLS, No. 1

Take one cake of cream cheese, one-quarter of a pound of chopped figs, one-quarter of a pound of chopped walnuts, roll into balls and serve on lettuce leaves.

CHEESE BALLS, No. 2

Mix one cake Neufchatel cheese, a piece of butter the size of the cheese, one tablespoon of cream, one-quarter teaspoon of salt and six dashes of Tabasco Sauce and form one large ball or several small ones and roll in chopped pecan nuts.

CHEESE SOUFFLÉ

Dissolve one and one-half tablespoons of butter, add one tablespoon of flour, stir until it loosens from the pan; add one and one-half cups of rich milk, pepper and salt. Take from the fire, add gradually four egg yolks and three-quarters of a cup of grated cheese, then the stiffly beaten whites of eggs. Bake in a hot oven in china ramekins about fifteen minutes and serve immediately.

CHEESE TIMBALS FOR TWELVE PEOPLE

Take one pint of milk, four tablespoons of flour, and use enough of the milk to dissolve the flour, the balance put in double boiler; when it boils, add the dissolved flour, then add one-quarter pound imported Swiss cheese grated. Let these two boil for fifteen minutes; when cool, add the yolks of four eggs; drop one in at a time and beat, then strain through a fine sieve about ten minutes before you put in the pans; beat the whites of two eggs and put in the above and mix; grease timbal forms, fill three-quarters full only; bake in pan of boiling water twenty minutes. Let them stand about two minutes, turn out on little plates, and serve with tomato sauce, a sprig of parsley put on top of each one.

WELSH RAREBIT

Melt one tablespoon of butter, add two cups finely cut American cheese, when it melts add one-half cup of milk or stale beer, keep stirring until it is smooth. Add one-half teaspoon of English mustard, two beaten eggs. Cook one minute longer and salt to taste. Serve on toast.

GOLDEN BUCK

One pound of cheese, one-eighth pound of butter, one-half glass of ale, one teaspoon of mustard, one egg (well beaten), and salt and paprika. Put butter in pan, and when melted add cheese cut up or grated; stir, and as cheese melts, add ale. When it begins to bubble, add egg well beaten. Stir continually to keep from getting stringy. In two or three minutes it will be ready to serve. Pour over hot buttered toast. This quantity is sufficient for four persons.

CHEESE BREAD

Take six thick slices of stale bread, well buttered; cut them in two; dip into milk; then place in a baking dish, with alternating layers of thinly sliced cheese, having cheese for top. Add half a cup of milk, into which a half teaspoon of dry mustard has been put. Bake in quick oven fifteen minutes. Serve at once.

GREEN CORN, TOMATOES AND CHEESE

Into one tablespoon of melted butter stir two cups of grated cheese until it, too, is melted. Add three-quarters of a cup of canned or grated fresh corn, one ripe green pepper, stir them, add one egg yolk mixed with one-half cup of tomato purée, one teaspoon of salt, one-half teaspoon of paprika. Toast five slices of bread and pour this mixture over it. Serve hot.

RICE AND CHEESE

Melt two ounces of butter in a stew-pan; fry in the buttery finely minced onion. When this is of a nice golden color stir into it a quarter of a pound of well-boiled rice. Work it well with a fork and then pour all into a buttered pie dish. Dredge over with a good coating of grated cheese, sprinkle the surface with melted butter and bake until nicely browned.

MACARONI AND CHEESE

Break three ounces of macaroni—noodles or spaghetti answer equally well—into small pieces, boil in rapidly boiling salted water; when tender drain off the water and add half a pint of milk; cook slowly till the macaroni has absorbed most of the milk. To half a pint of thick white sauce add two ounces of grated cheese and mix with the macaroni; last of all add two well-beaten eggs. Butter a pudding mold, sprinkle it with browned bread crumbs and pour in the macaroni mixture; steam gently for about half an hour, turn out and fill the centre with stewed tomatoes and mushrooms.

CHEESE OMELET

Cook in double boiler one cup of milk, add one tablespoon of butter, one tablespoon of flour blended together and cook till thick; one cup of cheese cut up added, and stir till dissolved. Remove from fire and stir in yolks of four eggs beaten, one-half teaspoon of salt (pepper). Fold in whites of four eggs beaten stiff and a pinch of baking powder. Bake in a buttered dish one-half hour.

CHEESE AND SWEET GREEN PEPPERS

Cheese and peppers make a very nice combination. Melt two ounces of cheese, add a tablespoon of chopped peppers and the same amount of butter, a little paprika, salt, and if liked, mustard. When the ingredients have been well blended pour the mixture on hot buttered toast and serve.

CHEESE FONDUE

Soak one-half cup of bread crumbs in one scant cup of milk; dissolve a speck of bicarbonate of soda in a drop of hot water and add to the milk, one egg, yolk and white beaten separately, one-half cup of dry cheese grated, one tablespoon of butter, salt and pepper to taste, beat well, pour into a well buttered baking dish, strew dry crumbs moistened with butter over the top, and bake in a hot oven until light brown. Serve at once in the dish in which it is baked.

TOMATOES, EGGS AND CHEESE (HUNGARIAN STYLE)

Place two tablespoons of butter in a pan (after having the water boil to heat the pan). Let butter melt, add one small onion chopped fine and cook until soft, a pint of tomatoes strained and let come to a boil; add one-half pound mild cheese cut fine; and stir until smooth. Break in three eggs and stir hard until eggs are done. Serve on buttered toast.

CRACKERS AND CHEESE

Split in two some Bent's water biscuits; moisten them with hot water and pour over each piece a little melted butter and French mustard; then spread with a thick layer of grated cheese; sprinkle with paprika or cayenne. Place them in a hot oven until the cheese is soft and creamy.

RAMEKINS OF EGG AND CHEESE

Beat three new-laid eggs and blend thoroughly with two ounces of grated cheese and one ounce of partly melted butter. Place the mixture in little pans or saucers and bake in the oven.

www.ingramcontent.com/pod-product-compliance
Lightning Source LLC
Chambersburg PA
CBHW081626100526
44590CB00021B/3627